RONALD SEARLE IN *LE MONDE*

Fin de siècle

RONALD SEARLE
IN *LE MONDE*

Ronald Searle

THE UNIVERSITY OF CHICAGO PRESS ● CHICAGO AND LONDON

RONALD SEARLE is a graphic artist, cartoonist, animator, and film designer. He is the author of dozens of books, most recently *The Terror of St. Trinian's and Other Drawings*. He has had one-man shows in New York, Philadelphia, San Francisco, and all over Europe, and his work is also found in the permanent collections of museums in London, New York, Paris, and Berlin, among others.

The University of Chicago Press, Chicago 60637

The University of Chicago Press, Ltd., London

Printed in the United States of America

11 10 09 08 07 06 05 04 03 02 1 2 3 4 5

ISBN: 0-226-74408-6 (cloth)

Library of Congress Cataloging-in-Publication Data

Searle, Ronald, 1920–

 Ronald Searle in Le Monde / Ronald Searle.

 p. cm.

 ISBN 0-226-74408-6

 1. Searle, Ronald, 1920– 2. World politics—1989– —Caricatures

and cartoons. 3. French wit and humor, Pictorial. 4. Editorial

cartoons—France. I. Monde. II. Title.

D860 .S4 2002

741.5'942—dc21

 2001007375

This book is printed on acid-free paper.

CONTENTS

Preface xi

POLITICS

MONEY

SOCIETY GAMES

SOME ANGELS

EPILOGUE

"QUI ÊTES VOUS, RONALD SEARLE?"

In my creaking eighties, after more than sixty years of publicly grappling with the peculiar nuances of graphic humor, I realize that, nevertheless, I am probably an unknown quantity to many of those who might encounter this book. So, for anyone interested in finding out who, or what, may be lurking behind the images on the following pages, a modest personal résumé follows.

The French have a neat way of tackling this situation on TV. The interviewer tosses the ball directly into the lap of the victim and poses the question *"Qui êtes vous?"* (Who are you?). Then, slumping back into his, or her, interrogation chair, lets the sweating unfortunate do the work. As the story unfolds, now is the time to reach for your box of tissues …

I was the first of two children born to a modest East-Anglian working-class family. Arbitrarily, fate stuck a pin into the map of England so that geographically and artistically, I was given an unexpectedly privileged start in life. Instead of being born in the bleak back-street of some grim industrial city, I arrived in the ancient university and agricultural town of Cambridge on the third of March 1920, in lodgings on the busy road to Newmarket racecourse.

During the First World War my mother, a country girl from Wiltshire in the south of England, had met and married my father, then a young professional soldier. At the time of my birth my father had been invalided out of the army. He was still recovering from the effects of poison gas and had returned, hardened and disillusioned, to his family roots in Cambridge. In a depressed postwar England he was now a twenty-three-year-old luggage porter on the local railway station, with a family to keep.

Postwar Cambridge, then a sleepy, underprivileged market town, had been dominated since the thirteenth century by its powerful, royally patronized university. In contrast with the modest means of the town, the university, a panorama of architectural splendor, boasted a number of richly endowed museums, and its seventeen colleges contained matchless libraries full of treasures.

Although they belonged to the university, the museums were open to the public and, throughout my childhood, my younger sister and I spent all our spare time soaking up the splendors and curiosities of these esoteric collections. Fascinated, we wandered among terrifying, ancient, bottled anatomical specimens and ethnographic rarities from university expeditions to the darker corners of the earth, such as shrunken human heads, monstrous stuffed beasts, as well as unspeakable objects from the

blackest of secret rituals. This was perhaps the cradle of the darker side of my sense of humor. Less gruesomely, there was also a rather intimidating museum of towering, dusty casts of classical Greek and Roman sculpture.

Above all there was the Fitzwilliam—a modestly sized museum of incredible richness with its ancient Egyptian sarcophagi, medieval armor, a world-renowned collection of Renaissance paintings, the remarkable assemblage of works by William Blake, as well as an impressive cabinet filled with brilliant watercolors by Turner. To us adolescents it was a revelation. Most unusually for a "serious" museum there was also a small room of contemporary caricatures, mainly devoted to Max Beerbohm, and it was here that my fascination with graphic humor was born and, soon after leaving school at the age of fifteen, I began contributing a primitive weekly cartoon to the local newspaper.

In addition to working—first as a parcel wrapper, then as a clerk—in a local emporium, I began to attend evening classes at the Cambridge School of Art. In 1938, after three years hard work, I fulfilled a dream. I was awarded a full-time art scholarship. But this pleasure was short-lived. By early 1939 the possibility of war became a reality and, along with my school friends, I volunteered to join the army reserve.

A few months later World War II was declared and—with a little album of the work of one of my heroes, the German satirist George Grosz, stuffed into the pocket of my uniform—I became a reluctant soldier for the next seven years. After an interminable spell of training and work on the art of camouflage for anywhere but the jungle, our brigade was shipped to the Far East in the winter of 1941. There we were to encounter the Japanese, who were now advancing down the Malayan peninsula. In February 1942, at the age of twenty-one, after several weeks of chaotic fighting, I was captured along with my friends. We remained prisoners of the Japanese for almost four years, spending a nightmarish time in the jungle of Thailand working on the so-called Death Railway and, among other things, on the construction of the notorious bridge on the river Kwai. Not surprisingly this baptism of cruelty and brutality by man toward man was to mark me and my work from then on.

Ultimately liberated from Changi prison in Singapore at the capitulation of Japan in 1945, skeletal, unwell, and penniless, I returned to an England that had totally changed. In 1946 I moved to London and set about earning my living as a freelance artist. Thanks to my bizarre, black, ex-prison humor and my by now fluent pen, I swiftly became noticed as being something different in the world of graphics. Soon I was not only working for European publications but was invited to become special features artist for such exotic magazines as *Holiday* and *Life* as well as eventually selling covers to the *New Yorker*. As a result of a solid academic training, my artistic range was almost unlimited and I was able to work in an extraordinary variety of fields: film animation for Hollywood, commemorative medal sculpting for the French Mint, book publishing in England, and, for a long time, I was the theatre caricaturist for *Punch*.

In 1961 I had left London to live in Paris, where I had met my future wife, Monica, a theatre and ballet designer. For the next few years, together, we traveled ceaselessly on international reportage, mostly for and in America. Then, reluctantly, in 1975, we had to leave Paris and resettle into a different life in the mountains of Provence.

The vast store of impressions and opinions that I had built up after years of traveling to record the vagaries of human na-

ture was now to serve me well. In 1995, I was offered the opportunity of contributing editorial drawings to the French national newspaper *Le Monde*.

For this aspect of graphic satire, erudition is not the most vital requirement. What is needed most is gut reaction to the *bêtises* of the human race. As man has yet to escape from the barbarian mentality still simmering beneath the thinnest of cultural veneers, subject matter is, unfortunately, always richly present. In an age when disasters, massacres, executions, and other miscellany of man's enlightened imagination are now mere TV news items to the vast majority of the public, it comes as no surprise that it is so difficult to reach a zone of human sensitivity beyond the TV screen.

After years of scratching away with a sharpish pen and countless buckets of ink, mostly in the well-ploughed field of light-hearted humor, it was fascinating to be offered an opportunity to change direction. The possibility of commenting on current events and, in particular, on those situations involving man's fatal propensity for self-destruction, is something that does not arise every day. When the offer to do precisely that came from a newspaper of such repute, I was halted in my tracks.

It is difficult to assess whether or not, in these days of computer-educated visual barbarians, satirical graphics can have the slightest impact on public opinion. On the whole I am pessimistic and fear that I am exercising a moribund art. But I push on hopefully—and will do so for as long as *Le Monde* will go on publishing the efforts.

For those who are not familiar with the nuances of the French press, *Le Monde* is a liberally minded afternoon newspaper, published from Paris since 1944 and now the most read and probably the most influential national daily in the country. For its fiftieth anniversary the paper was entirely rethought and redesigned. Among the innovations, in a paper noted for pages unsullied by any image, an exceptional amount of space was reserved for illustration and graphic comment. Although drawings and photographs are now tastefully spread throughout the paper, a four-column area on the main editorial page is the most desirable and fought over space. It was here, between 1995 and 2001, that the drawings appeared from which a selection was made for this book.

Drawings for this space are not solicited. There is no editorial pressure or guidance. It is left to the artist to seek and express his point of view. The editor either accepts it or returns the drawing. It is a tough exercise and a challenging one. Hopefully the effort involved remains hidden from the reader—but not the point of view.

Ronald Searle

January 2002

POLITICS

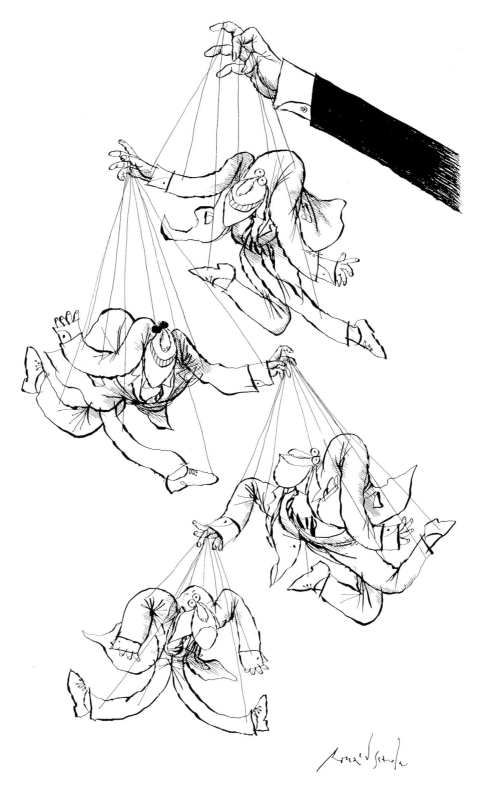

Who's pulling the strings?

Unraveling the election

Electoral battle of the Titans

Faux pas

Pouvoir

Power

The pact

The pact

Stalemate

The pact

The negotiators

The negotiator

Stalemate

Against the tide

Diplomacy

An honorable peace

Summit meeting

Diplomatic clarification

Dialogue of the deaf

Having a ball

20

Pandora

The judgment of Paris

Balance of power

EUROPE

Eurodance

Monetary union

Britain resists the Euro

Eurocynic Britannica

Euroskeptic Britannica

AFRICA

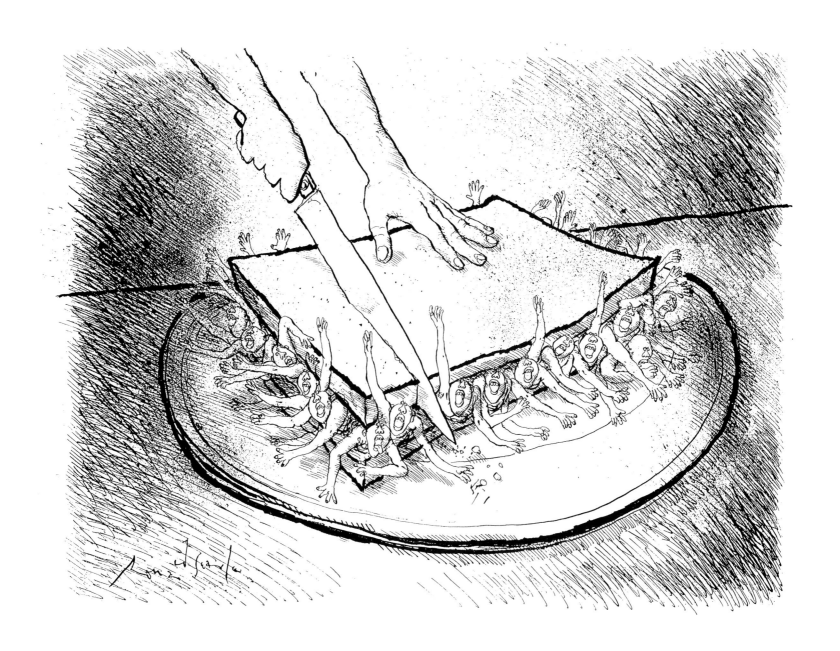

Sandwiched

Atlas

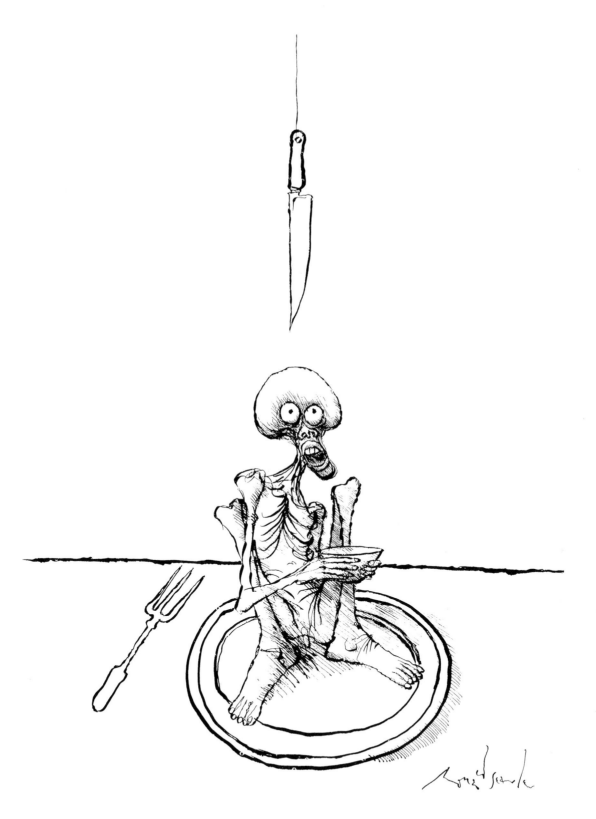

The knife of Damocles

Africa

In style

OTHER COUNTRIES, OTHER PROBLEMS

The world

The new Russia

Romulus and Mafius

Switzerland and confiscated Jewish property

Ireland: The 30-year war of bigotry

Afghanistan: The road to Paradise

To Be Continued...

Buckingham Dallas

Iranian tentacles

The Saddam line

Ubuhussein

Chopsticks: China plays around with Taiwan

Fin de siècle

MONEY

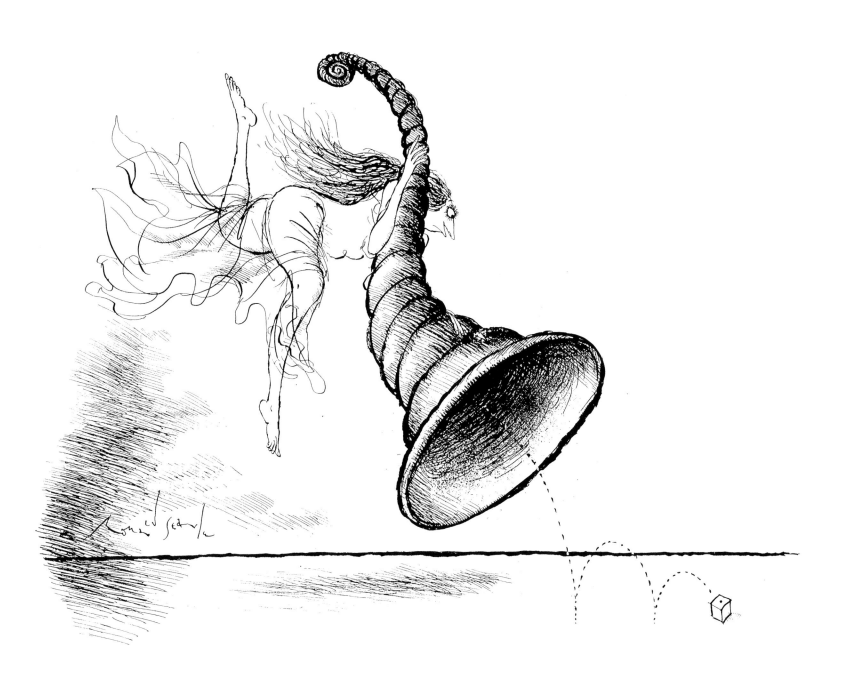

Recession

Snow White and the seven money launderers

Consumer society

Debit Lyonnais Bank

Business lunch

Party games

The golden calf

Crusade

Clintonstein's monster

Hullo holidays

Dream merchant

Vicious circle

SOCIETY GAMES

The dealer

Christmas

Children of the Gods

Football

Twilight of the Gods

Wheeler-dealers

The top

Friendly agreement

Influential person

Hierarchy

French law on the wing

Cult

Summer migration

Purgatory

Politically incorrect

Choice morsels

Christmas

The good life!

Bureaucratic stylites

Homo sapiens

WAR AND PEACE

Summit meeting

Phoenix

The buffoon

Swingtime

Glutton

See-Saw

Mercenaries

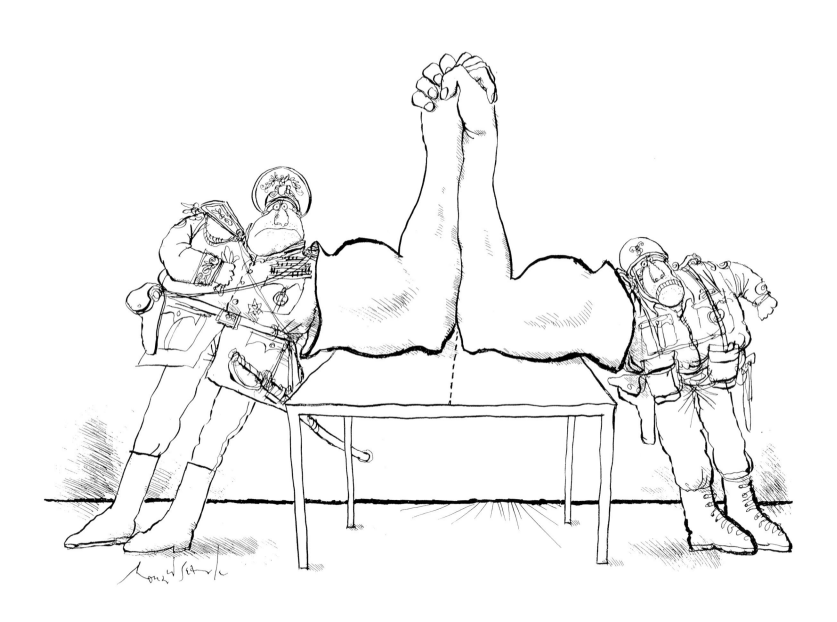

Only a small conflict

Provocation

Refugees

The tamer

Pygmalion

Beauty and the beast

War and Peace

Provisional peace

Killer kite

Timeout

Lottery—the winners

The big wash

Peace force

The winner!

Red carpet

Irresistible force meets immovable object

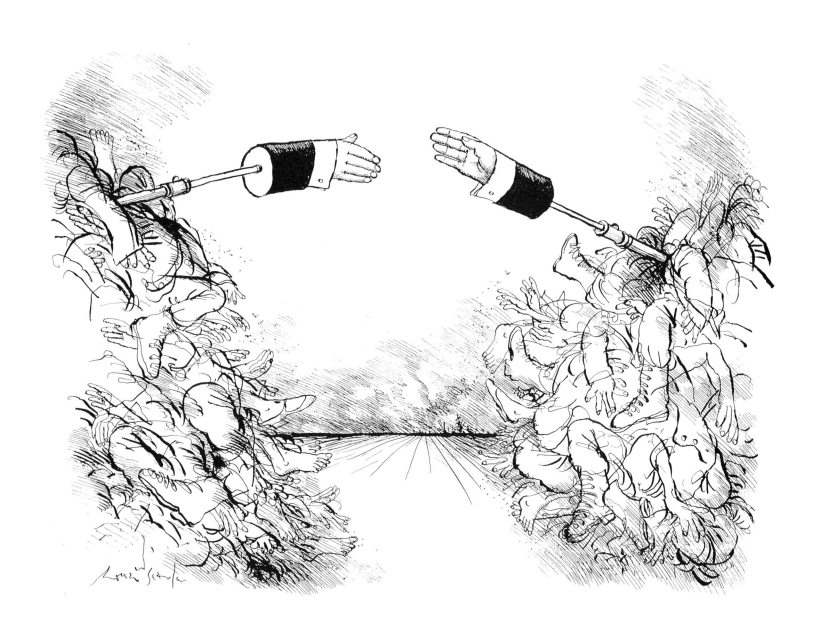

For the good of the people

In fashion

My God . . .

Carrousel

Tête-à-tête

Crocodile tears

The sensitive one

Pigeon of peace

Match without end

SOME ANGELS

Angel of peace

Angel of diplomacy

Angel of the third world

Angel of destiny

Angel of indifference

Angel of ignorance

Angel of pedophilia

Angel of politics

Angel of the stock exchange

Angel of minor conflicts

Angel of Munchausen syndrome

Angel of pollution

Angel of fast food

Angel of the vandals

Angel of plagiarism

Angel of parking

Angel of indecision

Angel of war

High treason

EPILOGUE

Liberty

Evolution

Clandestine immigration

Recession

Middle East: The Judgment of Solomon